Bobby Brewster Detective

With best wishes

from

H C Tull

and love from

BOBBY BREWSTER

Bobby Brewster Detective

H. E. TODD

illustrated by Lilian Buchanan

BROCKHAMPTON PRESS

SBN 340 03192 1

First printed 1964   Second impression 1969
Published by Brockhampton Press Ltd, Salisbury Road, Leicester
Printed in Great Britain by C. Tinling & Co. Ltd, Prescot
Text copyright © 1964 H. E. Todd
Illustrations copyright © 1964 Brockhampton Press Ltd

Contents

Introduction

Have you ever wanted to be a detective? I have, but I've never had the opportunity because I've been too busy doing other things.

Bobby Brewster was lucky because his chance to do some detecting came when he was still a boy — and an ordinary boy at that, even if his adventures are extraordinary.

Luckily he had Constable Wilkins to work with him, and the results of their efforts are shown in the first five chapters of this book.

I hope you like it.

H. E. TODD

International Private Investigator

The very first time he saw it in the shop Bobby Brewster decided that he simply must buy it as soon as he could. It was a smart-looking silver badge packed in a very important-looking black wallet. The badge was in the shape of a shield, with a star in the middle, and round the star were the impressive words 'International Private Investigator'. Inside the wallet was an identification card ready to be filled in by the owner, and in the pocket of the wallet was a notebook headed 'Investigations'.

Bobby Brewster longed to buy it and become an International Private Investigator himself. The only difficulty was that it cost 3/6d. and all he had in the world was 4½d. His next birthday was not for a long time and Christmas was three months after that, so there was very little chance of his being given the money he needed. There was only one thing to do. He would have to work for it.

Of course the right thing to do is always to help your mother and father without any idea of reward, isn't it, but Bobby thought there was no harm in his being extra helpful and hoping for the best. And it worked, too. First he was given sixpence by his father for weeding a large flower-bed in the garden – and Mr Brewster thought it was jolly well worth it. Then his mother allowed him to keep the change after he had carried a very heavy shopping basket for her one Saturday morning. That brought him up to 1/5d, and as he is always given ninepence a week, he was soon able to save the rest.

Bobby Brewster felt very excited on the morning he went to the shop, and he didn't mind handing over 3/6d in the least. He decided that to

be on the safe side he had better consult Constable Wilkins, a policeman friend of his, before filling in the identification card inside his wallet. After all, real International Private Investigators don't carry identification cards covered with crossings out and blots, do they? At least, I don't think they do.

Constable Wilkins was in the police-station. 'I'm very glad you're going to be an International Private Investigator, Bobby,' he said. 'You're not tall enough to join the police force, but the next best thing is to be a detective. We must always work together, and if you see anything suspicious be sure to report it to me, won't you?'

'Of course I will, Mr Wilkins,' said Bobby Brewster.

'As you are an International Private Investigator you may call me Constable Wilkins,' said Constable Wilkins.

'Thank you very much, Constable Wilkins,' said Bobby Brewster, and he felt most important.

They took great care to fill in the identity card properly, and when they had finished this is how it read:

NAME: Bobby Brewster

TOWN	COUNTY	COUNTRY
Harpenden	Hertfordshire	England

NATIONALITY: British

AGE: 8 years 3 months

HEIGHT: 4 feet 1½ inches WEIGHT: 4 stone 3 lbs.

COLOUR OF HAIR: Mousy. (I know that sounds silly, but it was Constable Wilkins's idea, because Bobby's hair is a sort of in between colour, neither fair or dark)

COLOUR OF EYES: Blue with yellow dots. (They are, really!)

DISTINGUISHING MARKS: Scar on knee. (Through falling off his bicycle)
Cut on left hand. (Through fiddling about with a penknife)
Spot on forehead. (Where he picked and it didn't get better)

IDENTITY NUMBER: 31/XST/45 (That was Constable Wilkins's idea, too. I don't know where he got it from)

RIGHT THUMB PRINT: (Luckily Bobby Brewster's thumb was dirty at the time so he didn't have to cover his thumb with ink before pressing it on the corner of the card)

PHOTOGRAPH: (He had his usual wide grin)

(Of course Bobby Brewster didn't actually write
all the extra bits that I have put in brackets on his
identification card. They are purely for your
information.) When it was finished he took out
the silver badge and put it in his buttonhole.

'I thought you were supposed to be an International *Private* Investigator,' said Constable
Wilkins.

'So I am,' said Bobby Brewster.

'There's nothing very private in wearing a
silver badge, is there?' said Constable Wilkins.

14

'Thieves and vagabonds will run a mile if they see that. Your badge is supposed to be kept in your wallet and only shown when you are actually investigating.'

'Oh, is it?' said Bobby Brewster, and secretly thought to himself 'That's a pity.'

Well, for the first week being an International Private Investigator wasn't very exciting because there was nothing to investigate. Bobby Brewster filled in his 'Investigations' notebook very carefully all the same –

MONDAY June 18th.   'Saw man fall off bike. Helped him get up. He said 'Thank you.'

TUESDAY June 19th.   'Nothing to report.'

WEDNESDAY June 20th.   'Chased Billy Singleton when he ran out of school. Asked him why he was hurrying. He said 'That's nothing to do with you.' Asked him again. He said 'I'm in a hurry.'

THURSDAY June 21st.   'Nothing to report.'

FRIDAY June 22nd. 'Mr Limcano had hay fever.'

SATURDAY June 23rd. 'My mother lost her front door key. Thought it might be stolen, but found it in her coat pocket.'

SUNDAY June 23rd. 'Mr Watson dropped the plate in church, and money rolled all over the place. Helped to pick it up.'

On that Sunday afternoon Bobby Brewster happened to meet Constable Wilkins and he showed him his notebook. Constable Wilkins read it through and said he didn't think there was anything suspicious enough to follow up, but he congratulated Bobby on making such careful notes. 'You never know when they might come in useful,' he said, and Bobby felt most flattered.

Then Constable Wilkins made a very exciting announcement.

'I don't know if you've heard,' he said, 'but last week there were a lot of robberies in the district. Someone has been walking into people's houses when they are out and stealing little things like coats and ornaments and odd change. And it's a funny thing. The thief always finishes by going into the kitchen and eating a meal of bread, cheese and pickles.'

'Oh, does he?' said Bobby Brewster, trying to look like a detective with an important clue.

'Yes,' said Constable Wilkins. 'Keep your eyes open, will you please? And report anything unusual you see or hear to me.'

'Certainly I will, Constable Wilkins,' said Bobby.

And that is how Detective Bobby Brewster started on his first case.

Bread, cheese and pickles

At first Detective Bobby Brewster decided to follow up the clue about the bread, cheese and pickles, but it was a waste of time. He asked lots of people if they were fond of bread, cheese and pickles, and if they said 'Yes' he made a note. Soon he had a long list in his notebook headed 'People who like bread, cheese and pickles,' but it wasn't much use to him. In the first place nearly all the people on the list were friends of his and he didn't think any of them was a thief – at least, he hoped not. In the second place the real thief would hardly own up to being fond of bread, cheese and pickles, would he? He would be far more likely to say 'No, I prefer hard-boiled eggs and lettuce,' just to be misleading.

Then, on the following Saturday morning, a very suspicious thing happened. Bobby didn't even realize it was suspicious at the time, so he took no notice. The dog next door started barking, and soon all the other dogs in the district joined in. The dog next door is a cheerful sort of shaggy mongrel called Frisky Henderson. He has an annoying habit of barking loudly about nothing, and the other dogs need very little encouragement to join in.

But later in the morning Mr and Mrs Henderson came home from their shopping, and the first thing they noticed was a plate on the kitchen table that had obviously been used by someone eating bread, cheese and pickles. Then they found that a thief had been in the house and that he had stolen some money and clothing as well as eating their bread, cheese and pickles, and that made them very annoyed. Of course they rang up the police-station and a policeman – not Constable Wilkins, but the local inspector – came to their house and took some notes. Bobby heard all about it when Mrs Henderson was talking to his mother in the garden later that morning.

Well, that was all very exciting, wasn't it? Bobby thought so, anyway, and he also thought that he must do something about it. After all, he wouldn't have been much of an International Private Investigator if he had done nothing, would he? The drawback was that there was nothing suspicious to see. The Henderson's house looked just the same as usual, and as it was a very hot day the thief had left no muddy footprints anywhere.

Then Bobby Brewster remembered the loud barking he had heard earlier in the morning, and he decided to try and find Frisky Henderson. That was more easily said than done, because Frisky is a wandering sort of dog. In the end he was found in a nearby field, and – this is a very important clue – in Frisky's mouth was a piece of material. Bobby called, but Frisky ran the other way. He always does when people call him, which is another annoying habit of his. Bobby sat down on the grass, and when Frisky approached with his tail wagging he was caught by the collar. At first when Bobby tried to take the piece of material, Frisky growled in a most alarming manner, but Bobby knew perfectly well it was only showing off. He threw a piece of stick a few yards away, and when Frisky pounced on it the piece of material fell to the ground.

It was a square piece of grey flannel. Bobby wondered how on earth Frisky had got hold of it.

'I shall have to report this to Constable Wilkins,' he said to himself. So he did.

Constable Wilkins was on his beat in the High Street. 'Hullo, Detective Brewster,' he said as Bobby ran up to him. 'What's the matter?'

'I've got something very important to report, Constable Wilkins,' said Bobby Brewster.

'What is it?' asked Constable Wilkins.

Bobby Brewster told him about the robbery at the Hendersons and the bread, cheese and pickles, and the loud barking, and the piece of material in Frisky's mouth.

'Now that is interesting,' said Constable Wilkins. 'Let me see the piece of material.'

Bobby gave it to him.

'Aha,' said Constable Wilkins. 'This looks like a piece out of some trousers. All we have to do is to find someone with a hole in his trousers exactly the same shape as this piece of material, and we've caught our man. You look this side of the road and I'll look that, and we'll meet at the war memorial.'

The High Street was crowded with shoppers that morning. It always is on a Saturday. Bobby tried to look at all the men's trousers, but it was a jolly difficult thing to do without getting in the way, and some of the people wondered what on earth he was playing at. One man got quite annoyed because Bobby stared rather hard at a patch on his trousers, but it wasn't a square patch and in any case it was made out of check material, so that was no good.

By the time Bobby met Constable Wilkins at

the war memorial he was tired out. 'It's no use,' he said. 'There isn't a hole to be seen anywhere.'

'You're not much of an International Private Investigator if you think you can solve your cases in half an hour,' said Constable Wilkins. 'We must go on trying.'

At that moment Detective Bobby Brewster had a brilliant idea.

'Did you hear the weather forecast this morning?' he asked.

'As a matter of fact I did,' said Constable

Wilkins. 'It's going to be fine and very hot all day.'

'That's what I thought,' said Bobby. 'Then why is that little man over the other side of the road wearing a heavy overcoat that is much too big for him? He looks silly to me.'

'He does indeed,' said Constable Wilkins. 'He must have something to hide. I think we'd better investigate.' So they both walked over the road.

'Good morning,' said Constable Wilkins to the little man in the big overcoat.

'Good morning, mate,' said the little man in the big overcoat, looking rather startled.

'You look tired,' said Constable Wilkins. 'If you wear a heavy overcoat like that on a hot day like this you might faint.'

'Not me, mate,' said the little man. 'I've never fainted in me life.'

'I think you'd better take off your overcoat all the same,' said Constable Wilkins.

'I might catch cold,' said the little man.

'You might catch something worse than that if you don't do as I tell you,' said Constable Wilkins, looking very fierce.

24

The little man took off his overcoat quickly and Constable Wilkins felt in the pockets.

'Now turn round,' said Constable Wilkins.

The little man turned round. There was a large square hole in the seat of his grey flannel trousers.

'Now you know why I was wearing an overcoat,' said the little man with a nervous laugh.

'Yes,' said Constable Wilkins. 'But I still don't know why you were carrying this in your pocket.' And he held out a brown paper bag.

What do you think was in it? A crust of bread, a piece of cheese, and a small bottle of pickles.

Well, that was most suspicious, wasn't it? Constable Wilkins thought so, anyway. He asked the little man to accompany him to the police-station, where, after a few more questions, the little man owned up to all the robberies.

And that is how Detective Bobby Brewster helped to solve the case of the Bread, Cheese and Pickles robberies. And you can be quite sure that it made him all the more determined to carry on with his investigations as an International Private Detective.

Follow that spider

It's a jolly good thing for the Hendersons that they
live next door to Detective Bobby Brewster.
If they didn't their house would soon be nearly
empty because since the cheese and pickles affair
they've had some more robberies. They have,
really. And, what's more, they were some of the
most extraordinary robberies that can ever have
happened, as I am sure you will agree when you
have read this story.

A few weeks ago Bobby Brewster went to the Hendersons for tea, and when it was over Mr Henderson said —

'Now Bobby, I must introduce you to our spider.'

'Your spider?' asked Bobby Brewster.

'Yes,' said Mr Henderson. 'We have a spider that spends most of its time inside the lock of our back door. Let's go and see if it's there now.'

They did, and it was. Mr Henderson turned the handle of the door and the spider came scuttling out of the keyhole. An ugly-looking creature it was, too, with lots of hairy legs and two bulging eyes. Bobby Brewster thought to himself that if it had lived in *his* back door lock, he would have kept quiet about it and not introduced it to visitors.

Well, after that he thought no more about it for a week or two, until one morning he met Constable Wilkins out on his beat.

'Ah, I'm glad I met you, Detective Brewster,' said Constable Wilkins. 'I want you to keep your eyes open. Your neighbours, the Hendersons, are in trouble again. They've reported to me that things are disappearing from their house.'

'What sort of things?' asked Bobby Brewster.

'Oh, small things like silver salt-cellars and spoons and watches and pieces of cheese,' said Constable Wilkins.

'Pieces of cheese, did you say?' asked Bobby Brewster in surprise.

'Yes,' said Constable Wilkins. 'They seem to be very unlucky with cheese in that house. And there's another funny thing. Every night they lock all their doors carefully, but every morning they find their back door open.'

'You're sure it's the *back* door?' asked Bobby Brewster.

'Positive,' said Constable Wilkins. 'They showed it to me first thing this morning. Why do you ask?'

'Because a spider lives in the lock of the Henderson's back door,' said Bobby. 'They introduced me to it when I went to tea the other day.'

'Did they indeed,' said Constable Wilkins. 'But I don't see what that has to do with it. What use could a silver salt-cellar possibly be to a spider?'

'None at all,' said Bobby Brewster, 'But you never know. Anyway, I'll keep my eyes open as you said.'

So he did, but saw nothing for several days until, one Saturday morning, a very funny thing happened. Bobby had taken a message from his mother to Mrs Henderson, when he noticed a spider scuttling away from their back door. He watched it carefully. The spider scuttled through a hole in the fence and down the bank on the other side. Lying on the ground was a man trying to hide. Bobby crouched down behind the fence, and saw the spider crawl right up to the man. Then the man leant over and, believe it or not, started whispering to the spider. He did, really. It was too far away to hear much, but Bobby heard one whispered word quite distinctly —

'*Tonight.*'

Then the man glanced round to make sure nobody was looking (I wonder what he would have done if he had seen Bobby?), and the spider

scuttled quickly back to the Henderson's house.

Well, thought Bobby to himself, I suppose I'd better report this as soon as I can.

Constable Wilkins was out on his beat again and Bobby soon found him.

'I know it sounds silly,' said Bobby, 'but I think that spider *has* got something to do with the robberies at the Henderson's. I followed it today and it went to see a very suspicious-looking man.'

'What happened then?' asked Constable Wilkins.

'The man started talking to it,' said Bobby.

'I beg your pardon?' asked Constable Wilkins.

'I said the man started talking to it,' said Bobby.

'He did, really. I couldn't hear most of what he said, but I did hear one word. It was "Tonight".'

'Did you indeed?' said Constable Wilkins. 'Well, that settles it. It's probably a waste of time, but I'll hide in the Henderson's back garden tonight and see what happens.'

So he did – and it wasn't a waste of time at all. At about one o'clock in the morning, when all was quiet, a suspicious-looking man crept silently up to the Henderson's back door. He switched on a torch and Constable Wilkins saw the spider crawl out of the keyhole. There were whispered words.

'It's open,' someone said. Then, in spite of the fact that the Hendersons had been heard to lock their back door before going to bed, the man turned the handle and walked in.

Frisky Henderson didn't even have the sense to bark. He came running up to the man with his tail wagging, and licked his hand as if to say 'I'm *so* glad you've come. Do come in and help yourself.' Which is exactly what the man did, while the spider kept watch at the back door.

After that things moved quickly. Luckily Constable Wilkins had arranged for another policeman to be hiding with him in the back garden. They crept towards the door and in a very short time the man came back carrying a sack over his shoulder. He stooped to whisper to the spider, and, like a flash, the other policeman pounced on the thief, and Constable Wilkins covered the spider with a box.

So they were both caught red-handed, and as the man's sack was full of silver candlesticks, fish-knives and forks, and pieces of cheese, there was complete proof of their guilt.

Well, as you can imagine, the affair caused quite a stir. The case was heard at the local sessions before Mr Justice Jackson. Mr Justice Jackson is an elderly judge with a twinkle in his eye, who looks like a good-natured tortoise with spectacles.

The court rose respectfully when the judge entered and he looked around and said, 'Mr Clerk, I understood there were two accused in this case. Thomas Blenkinsopp and Samuel Spider. I can only see one in the dock. Where's the other?'

'In that box on the dock rail, m'lud,' said the clerk of the court.

'I beg your pardon?' asked Mr Justice Jackson.

'I said in that box, m'lud,' said the clerk of the court. 'Thomas Blenkinsopp is the accused you

can see, and if you'll peep through the holes in the box, you'll also see Samuel Spider.'

The box was handed to the judge.

'Bless my soul,' he said. 'Samuel really is a spider. And do the accused plead guilty or not guilty?'

'Guilty,' said Thomas Blenkinsopp.

'Guilty,' said a voice from inside the box, and the judge said 'Bless my soul' again.

All the evidence was quite clear, although some of it was very surprising. Detective Bobby Brewster and Constable Wilkins were both complimented on their smart detection work, and the jury only took two minutes to find the accused 'Guilty.'

'Before passing sentence,' said the judge, 'I wish to satisfy myself about one thing. Who was the ringleader in these robberies? Thomas Blenkin-sopp, I wish to know how on earth you first got into conversation with the – er – spider.'

'I didn't, your Honour,' said the accused. 'He got into conversation with me.'

'I see,' said the judge. 'How did this happen?'

'I was asleep in the grass at the bottom of the bank one morning when a voice whispered in my ear the word "Cheese".'

'Cheese, did you say?' asked Mr Justice Jackson.

'Yes, your Honour,' said Thomas Blenkinsopp. 'I woke up and there was the spider.'

'What were your reactions?' asked the judge.

'I was very surprised to hear a spider whispering,' said Thomas Blenkinsopp.

'I'm sure you were,' said the judge. 'Especially a word like cheese. And what else did he say?'

'I can't remember his actual words,' said Blenkinsopp, 'but what it boiled down to was that the spider promised to open the Henderson's door for me to go and steal their silver on condition that I stole their cheese for him to eat.'

'Couldn't he have stolen the cheese for himself?' asked Mr Justice Jackson.

'No, your Honour,' said Blenkinsopp. 'They keep it under cover on a cheese dish.'

'I see,' said the judge. 'Well, it seems to me that you've been sadly led astray, and so I propose to deal lightly with you. Thomas Blenkinsopp, you will be bound over to be of good behaviour, but, I warn you, you must *not* get into conversation with spiders, do you hear?'

'Yes, your Honour,' said Blenkinsopp, looking very relieved. 'I promise that if I ever so much as see a spider, I'll run away.'

'Very good,' said Mr Justice Jackson. Then he turned to the box on the dock rail.

'Samuel Spider,' he said severely, 'you are the really guilty one in this case. You've used your undoubted talents in a criminal manner, and you must pay for it. I can't send you to prison because you'd only crawl out again. But you must be confined in some way. I order you to remain inside that box in the custody of Constable Wilkins until such a time as he's satisfied that you're a reformed character. Constable Wilkins, do you know what spiders eat?'

'Never having kept one as a pet, I can't say I do, your Honour,' said Constable Wilkins, scratching his head.

'Cheese,' said a voice from inside the box.

'There's your answer,' said Mr Justice Jackson. 'Since this passion for cheese has been his undoing, you'll feed Samuel spider on nothing but cheese until he's so sick of it he promises to be good.'

36

'Very well, your Honour,' said Constable Wilkins, and the court adjourned.

Well – the story ends quite happily after all. Thomas Blenkinsopp has found a job as a night-watchman and is a useful member of society. As for Samuel Spider, he soon got on so well with Constable Wilkins that he has been let out of his box and now lives in the front door lock at the police-station. Indeed, he is almost a member of the force, because they find him very useful in cases where doors need to be unlocked because the keys have been lost.

I told you at the beginning of this story that it was about one of the most extraordinary robberies that have ever happened. I was right, wasn't I?

Pork chops

The poor old Hendersons have been in trouble again. They have, really. Not serious trouble, but annoying for both of them.

We'll start with Mrs Henderson. She is a very proud housewife and a good cook, and one Sunday not long ago was their wedding anniversary, so she cooked her husband his favourite lunch. Pork chops. Lovely they were, with crackling done to a turn.

When they were ready she went out to the garden and called, 'Charles dear, lunch is ready.' But it wasn't. As Mr Henderson came towards the house he heard a scream. He ran into the kitchen calling, 'What's the matter?' and found his wife looking very red in the face.

'Someone's eaten our pork chops,' she said.

Mr Henderson ran out of the back door. 'Who's there?' he cried – though why he should expect anyone who had been eating his pork chops to answer 'Me' I can't imagine.

Mr Brewster was on the other side of the fence.

'I'm here,' he called. 'What do you want?'

'Have you seen a suspicious-looking character running out of our house?' asked Mr Henderson.

'No,' said Mr Brewster. 'Why do you ask?'

'Because someone's been in our kitchen and eaten our pork chops,' said Mr Henderson.

'I say, that's bad luck,' said Mr Brewster. 'What will you have for lunch?'

'I don't know,' said Mr Henderson. 'Bread and cheese, I suppose.'

'We can't allow that,' said Mr Brewster. 'You

must come and have lunch with us. I'm sure our joint is large enough for two extra. I bought it myself yesterday. Roast beef.'

Mr Henderson had been about to protest that it really wasn't necessary, but the bit about the roast beef made him change his mind. So both men went and had a word with their wives and it was all arranged.

Having the Hendersons for lunch was quite a treat for Bobby Brewster. They are not the sort of neighbours who are always popping in (much to Mrs Brewster's relief) and it made a change. Besides, a lot of the talk at table was about the mysterious disappearance of the pork chops, and that was very interesting to Detective Bobby Brewster.

'Here's your chance to do some more detective work, Bobby,' said Mr Henderson. 'You helped to catch the thief who stole our cheese and pickles. Now you must solve the case of our pork chops.'

Bobby felt most important and immediately after lunch was over he went with Mrs Henderson into her kitchen to investigate.

There was no clue to be found there, even with the magnifying glass which he always carries when he is investigating. The empty dish covered with gravy stains stood on the table, but there were no footprints or greasy finger-marks anywhere. Bobby was just going to give it up as a bad job when Mr Henderson came running in – and he was even redder in the face than his wife had been when she first found the pork chops were missing.

'More trouble,' he said, puffing hard.

'Whatever's the matter this time?' asked Mrs Henderson.

'You know those beautiful asters growing in our back garden,' said Mr Henderson.

'Yes,' replied his wife.

'Well, they're not beautiful any more,' said Mr Henderson. 'Someone's dug them up and smashed them.'

'Whoever would want to do a thing like that?' cried Mrs Henderson indignantly.

'I can't imagine,' said Mr Henderson.

'Could it be that horrid Mr Maynard?' suggested Mrs Henderson. 'He's always jealous of your beautiful garden, especially when you win all the prizes at the flower-show.'

'He's on holiday in Scotland,' said Mr Henderson. 'So he can't have done it – although I wouldn't put it past him if he was at home.'

'Have you any other jealous neighbours?' inquired Detective Bobby Brewster in an intelligent voice.

'Not that I know of,' said Mr Henderson. 'Besides, why didn't they dig up the flowers in the front garden? They're much easier to get at.'

'Yes, I suppose that's true,' said Bobby, looking

very thoughtful. 'Well – I'd better go and investigate at once.'

So he did – but he found nothing. The flower bed in the Henderson's back garden was certainly in an awful mess, but once again there were no signs of footprints. Nor was there a break in the fence where someone might have forced a way in.

When Bobby went to the back of the garden who should he see but Frisky Henderson. Frisky by name, and frisky by nature. He is a silly, cheerful dog who lollops about barking at nothing and getting into people's way. But that afternoon he wasn't lolloping about. He wasn't even barking for once. He was fast asleep on the muck heap – which is just the sort of silly place he would choose to sleep.

Now during the day Frisky does not often sleep unless he has had a big meal, and that is given to him in the evening. But what made Detective Bobby Brewster even more suspicious was Frisky's nose. He was lying in a stupor with his nose tucked under his tummy. And Frisky's nose was COVERED WITH MUD.

Bobby thought very hard. He didn't want to cause any trouble without being certain, but at the same time he didn't want the Hendersons to go on thinking that they had jealous neighbours who dug up their flowers. So he kept a very close watch on the muck heap.

Later that afternoon, just before his supper time, Frisky woke up and came running to the house in his usual gormless way. Mrs Henderson met him at the back door and talked to him in the doggie voice she will always persist in using.

'Frisky darling,' she cried. 'What *has* my poor little doggie been doing? All covered in mud and cabbage leaves?' Little did she guess. Frisky looked a picture of injured innocence, so Mrs Henderson went on with her doggie talk.

'Time for Frisky's din – dins,' she said. 'Frisky come into Mummy's kitchen and Mummy will give it to him.'

Frisky went into Mummy's kitchen, and Mummy *did* give it to him. A huge plate piled with dog food it was. How on earth Frisky could face it after his earlier exploits I don't know, but he did. He gobbled it up with great relish. And that wasn't all. When he had finished it he thought he would have a second course. So he ran out of the back door and straight to the flower bed.

It was at that moment that Bobby Brewster went to find Mr Henderson, who was reading a paper in the sitting-room.

'Mr Henderson,' said Bobby, 'I think I've solved both mysteries in one.'

'Whatever do you mean?' asked Mr Henderson.

'Look out of the back window at your flower bed,' said Bobby. Mr Henderson looked, and there was Frisky digging for all his worth among the asters.

'Frisky, what are you doing?' cried Mr Henderson. Frisky looked up in a guilty way, but then went on digging. And before Mr Henderson could get out of the french window, Frisky had dug up two pork chop bones and was running away down the garden with them as fast as he could go.

Well – that was that, wasn't it? The case of the stolen pork chops and the case of the broken asters were both solved at once. As you can imagine, Mr Henderson was very grateful to Detective Bobby Brewster for his help. But he wasn't at all pleased with Frisky, and when he managed to catch him later that evening he said so in no uncertain fashion.

Don't worry sheep

Bobby Brewster sometimes wonders if Frisky
Henderson can ever be taught to behave like a
sensible dog. The trouble is that he's so scatter-
brained – that is, if he has any brains to scatter.
And yet you can't help liking the animal. He
comes lolloping up with a doggy grin on his face
and his tail wagging like mad. He is so obviously
delighted to see you, and takes it for granted that
you are just as delighted to see him. You usually

47

are too, until he does something silly – like knocking you down, or rolling in a muck heap and then jumping on the sitting-room sofa and rolling on that too. As a watchdog he is useless, because he's either fast asleep or, when awake, ready to welcome anybody to the house, friend or stranger, day or night.

For a few days after Mr Henderson had spoken to him sharply about stealing the pork chops and burying those in the flower bed, Frisky was quite subdued. Bobby wondered if at last he had learned sense. But he hadn't, as you will soon see.

It isn't exactly a detective story this time, because the crime was so obvious that it needed no detection. It all started when Detective Bobby Brewster met Constable Wilkins on his beat one morning.

'Good morning, Constable Wilkins,' said Bobby Brewster.

'Good morning, Detective Brewster,' said Constable Wilkins.

'Do you need any help this morning?' asked Bobby.

'Well yes, as a matter of fact I do,' said Constable Wilkins. 'Farmer Dickens has reported to me that a local dog has been worrying his sheep. He's told me that I must warn the owner that he'll shoot the animal if he catches it.'

'And who is the dog's owner?' asked Bobby.

'I'm not absolutely sure,' said Constable Wilkins. 'But I know he lives near here, and I have a suspicion that the dog belongs to —'

'Don't tell me,' broke in Bobby. 'I can guess. It's Frisky Henderson, the dog next door.'

'That's right,' said Constable Wilkins. 'How did you know?'

'If anyone ever complains about a dog being naughty, I think straight away of Frisky Henderson,' said Bobby. 'He's the silliest dog that ever wagged a tail.'

'Well, his tail won't wag much longer unless he learns to behave himself,' said Constable Wilkins. 'Farmer Dickens means business.'

'Perhaps we'd better investigate and see what can be done about it,' suggested Bobby.

'Yes,' agreed Constable Wilkins. 'The sheep

are grazing in Dickens's field this morning. We'll go there straight away.'

Have you ever stopped and really listened to a lot of sheep *baaing*? It really is a most absurd noise. And yet it sounds quite like a lot of people talking – which probably explains why you sometimes hear one person say to another, 'I *do* wish you'd stop bleating.'

All the sheep were bleating that morning, but four of them were in particularly good voice. Either they were father, mother, son and daughter, or members of the same choir. One had a great deep bass voice. BAW – like that. Then there was the tenor who sounded as if he might at any moment break into a song like, 'Take a pair of sparkling eyes.' But he didn't. He just said BAAH. Then the rather demure mother was trying to be soothing – BAA. And last of all a pathetic little treble bleat from sister sheep – BEEAAH. Then back to father sheep. And so on. Not once, but again and again.

BAW	BAAH	BAA	BEEAAH
Bass	Tenor	Alto	Treble
BAW	BAAH	BAA	BEEAAH
Father	Son	Mother	Daughter

Then suddenly there sounded a note of alarm. Some sheep near the hedge started running towards the middle of the field, panicking and barging into each other. Silly sheep by name and silly sheep by nature. The sheep in the middle looked sharply towards the gate, and who do you think bounded in – all full of enthusiasm and high spirits?

Frisky Henderson, of course.

He didn't mean any harm. He wanted to play with the sheep, and when they ran away he thought they were playing with him. So he

barked at them, and darted backwards and for-
wards. Then he sat on his haunches breathing
heavily, with his tongue hanging out and a
mischievous expression on his face. Then another
dart forward, and more barking.

Of course, the poor sheep were terrified. They
lurched away as if they were being attacked by a
man-eating tiger, instead of being played with by
silly, harmless Frisky Henderson.

'First we must catch him – then decide what to
do with him,' said Constable Wilkins. 'If he goes
on barking like that, Farmer Dickens will soon be
coming with his gun.'

Constable Wilkins and Bobby Brewster ad-
vanced towards the middle of the field, the policeman round one way and Bobby round the other.
Then Bobby called Frisky and the usual business
started. Frisky Henderson has never been known
to do what he is told – and on this occasion he did
just the opposite. When Bobby shouted, 'Come
here,' he went there. But he didn't know Constable Wilkins was just behind him waiting to
grab his collar, and so he was caught.

'Now what shall we do?' asked Bobby, running up.

'It's no good taking him home for a good talking to,' said Constable Wilkins. 'By the time Mr Henderson does the talking the dog will have forgotten all about the sheep. He must be dealt with on the spot.'

Then Bobby Brewster had an idea.

'Frisky has been worrying the sheep,' he said. 'What about the sheep worrying Frisky for a change?'

'What do you mean?' asked Constable Wilkins.

'There's a sheep pen over there,' said Bobby. 'Let's put Frisky into it and make sure he doesn't get out. Then instead of Frisky barking at the sheep, the sheep can bleat at Frisky. They sound so silly that he'll soon want to have nothing more to do with sheep.'

And that is what they did. They dragged Frisky, protesting violently, into the pen and closed it round him. All the sheep were very interested to see a dog inside it, instead of being herded into it themselves. Especially the four singers.

BAW	BAAH	BAA	BEEAAH
Bass	Tenor	Alto	Treble

BAW	BAAH	BAA	BEEAAH
Father	Son	Mother	Daughter

And so on. Not once, but again and again.

At first Frisky barked back. But it had no effect at all and the bleating continued.

BAW   BAAH   BAA   BEEAAH

Frisky lay down and pushed his nose under his tummy, with one eye open.

BAW   BAAH   BAA   BEEAAH

Frisky covered his ears with his paws and a pathetic look of appeal came into his face. But Constable Wilkins and Bobby Brewster had no mercy. There he was and there he stayed. A silly dog being worried by some even sillier sheep.

When at last they thought he had had enough, they let Frisky out of the sheep pen. But he didn't bound out in his usual way. He slunk back home with his tail between his legs, and from that day to this, Farmer Dickens has never had to complain about dogs worrying his sheep. And, what's more, whenever Frisky Henderson sees a sheep, even a baby sheep, he runs the other way.

Dolls are for girls

Bobby Brewster has a young cousin called Barbara Brewster. She is a very nice girl, although sometimes she giggles too much. After all, there's nothing unusual about that, is there? Doesn't your young sister sometimes giggle too much? Or, for that matter, don't you?

Barbara lives in the north of Ireland and often comes to stay at Bobby's home. She usually comes during the school holiday, but last December Bobby had several days of his term still to go when she arrived, because for some reason or other her school had broken up early.

When Bobby came home from school on the first day of her visit, Barbara was waiting for him in the hall. He said 'Hullo, Barbara, I'm glad to see you,' in a lordly sort of way, just to show that he was a boy and one month older. Barbara was obviously excited and she took him by the hand.

'Bobby, I've got something *marvellous* to show you,' she cried, and she led him up to her bedroom. There, lying on the bed, were ten small dolls, all beautifully dressed in national costumes.

'Here, aren't they lovely?' she cried.

Bobby tried to look superior, but actually only succeeded in looking rather silly.

'They're all right, I suppose,' he said, 'but dolls are for girls.'

'These aren't just ordinary dolls,' said Barbara. 'Can't you see they all come from different countries? Look at the pretty clothes they are wearing, from Japan, and China, and India and

Spain, and all sorts of exciting places. I bet you've never seen such a lovely collection of dolls.'

'I've never looked,' said Bobby Brewster. 'As I said before, dolls are for girls.'

Then he thought to himself that perhaps he was being rather rude. After all, Barbara had only just arrived for her visit, and he didn't want to start arguing right from the start, did he, even if she was only a girl and one month younger.

'I don't want to be unkind, Barbara,' he said. 'As a matter of fact, they're jolly good dolls as dolls go. But what *use* are they, just lying there looking pretty?'

'Looking pretty *is* useful to start with,' said Barbara, 'because it cheers people up. And besides, since I started collecting these dolls, I've learned all about their homes and the lives they lead, and this term I was top in geography.'

'Oh, were you?' said Bobby. His results had not come out yet, but he thought that with luck he might be about tenth, so he kept quiet about it.

'Who do you like best?' asked Barbara.

'I really don't know yet,' said Bobby Brewster. 'I suppose they all have names. Perhaps you'd better introduce them to me before I decide.'

'Certainly,' said Barbara. 'The Chinese girl is called Cheeling; Gretel has long, fair plaits and comes from Holland. The lassie with the kilt is Janet, and you know where she comes from, don't you?

'Hans is the only boy. He wears breeches with smart braces and he has a smile on his face and a feather in his hat and comes from Austria. The Red Indian squaw has a beautiful name which I can't pronounce, and it means Whispering Pines. This is Sarah from the Channel Islands, and that is Gwynneth who is a Welsh girl. You can see that Malulah is an Indian because she wears a lovely sari. Carla has black, flashing eyes and comes from Spain, and last but not least, the little Japanese girl is Sugar Flower.'

'You've certainly chosen pretty names for them,' said Bobby. 'And I must admit they all look quite nice, but surely you can guess who I like best, can't you?'

'Who?' asked Barbara.

'Hans, of course,' said Bobby Brewster. 'The smiling boy with the feather in his hat.'

'You *would* choose a boy,' said Barbara.

'Naturally,' said Bobby. 'After all, I'm one myself, and boys are much more sensible than girls.'

'Oh no, they're not,' cried Barbara.

'Oh yes, they are,' said Bobby Brewster.

'I don't think so,' said Barbara.

'Well, I do,' said Bobby – and I really think they would still be arguing if at that moment they had not been called downstairs to tea.

Of course, they didn't argue at tea. For one thing Mrs Brewster would never have allowed it, and for another they were far too busy eating – can you guess what? Sardine sandwiches.

After tea Barbara insisted on helping her aunt wash up. Bobby felt rather ashamed about this, because he never actually offers to help with the washing up. Sometimes his mother asks him to, and even then he often pretends he has more important things to do, although he never gets away with it. On this occasion he cleared away the clean things and folded the table-cloth without any questions. His mother raised her eyebrows when she realized what was happening, but she was wise enough not to say anything.

When they had finished tea Barbara drew Bobby aside.

'I don't want to bore you, Bobby,' she said, 'but there's something more to tell you about my dolls. They're magic.'

'I beg your pardon?' asked Bobby Brewster.

'I said my dolls are magic,' whispered Barbara mysteriously. 'When I go to bed I always take one of them into bed with me – a different one each night – while the others sleep on the chair.'

'There's nothing magic about that,' said Bobby. '*You* do it, not the dolls.'

'Ah, but you see,' said Barbara, 'in the morning the doll in bed with me – whichever one it is – always wakes me up.'

'How?' asked Bobby Brewster.

'In different ways,' said Barbara. 'For instance, Janet plays the bagpipes, Carla does a Spanish dance on my tummy, and Whispering Pines puts a finger in her mouth and does the Red Indian Whoop, like this — W – H – O – O – O – P.'

'I don't believe you,' said Bobby Brewster. 'You must be dreaming it.'

'Oh no, I'm not,' said Barbara. 'It's true, and it's jolly useful too, because nowadays I always get up in time and never have to rush over my dressing.'

Well, Bobby was not at all convinced about the magic business, but for once he could see no point in arguing about it, so he decided to keep quiet.

Then the next morning, a very funny thing happened. It was the day of the arithmetic exam, and Bobby took his satchel to school with all the things he needed. The boys trooped into the classroom sharp at nine o'clock, and for once they looked serious because they had a funny, excited sort of exam feeling in their tummies. You know the feeling I mean. Nice but awful. The first thing they did was to lay their pencils, pens and rulers tidily on their desks, and can you guess what Bobby Brewster found in his satchel? Hans, the smiling boy with the feather in his hat. He did, really! He tried to slip Hans quickly back into his satchel before the other boys noticed, but he was too late, because Mr Limcano said:

'Ah, I see Bobby Brewster has brought his mascot with him.'

All the boys laughed much more loudly than necessary because they were relieved to have something to laugh at at such a serious time, but Mr Limcano soon put a stop to that.

'There's no need to laugh, boys,' he said. 'If Bobby Brewster thinks that his mascot will bring him luck, he was very sensible to bring it.'

So then Bobby had no alternative but to keep Hans on his desk, had he? And, do you know, it's a very funny thing, but Hans really *did* help

Bobby with his examination. Of course, he didn't actually say anything, but when Bobby came to a difficult question, he looked at Hans's smiling face, and that helped him to remember what he had been taught. By the end of the morning Bobby wasn't tired and he felt quite ready for the history examination in the afternoon.

Of course, as they were leaving at dinner-time one of the boys tried to be funny. I'm not sure which one – probably Billy Singleton. He passed Bobby Brewster a note which said —

'Bobby Brewster had a doll which followed him to
  school.

It went with Bobby everywhere and made him look
a fool.'

64

Then, as if that wasn't enough, the note went on to say —

'Even if they haven't got curls
Dolls aren't for boys, they're for girls.'

Bobby Brewster took no notice. He went home to dinner, and when Barbara asked him how he had got on he replied 'Oh, fine, thanks to you for putting Hans in my satchel.'

'Whatever do you mean?' asked Barbara. 'I've been looking for Hans all the morning. I didn't put him in your satchel.'

Bobby felt rather puzzled.

'Well, anyway,' he said, 'he's a jolly good exam mascot. Will you do me a favour and let me borrow him for my history exam this afternoon?'

'Certainly,' said Barbara, so it was all arranged. And later, when the marks for his examinations were announced, Bobby found he had done much better than expected. He wasn't top, of course, because he isn't all that clever, but he was in the first half of the class. And the remarks on his report were a great improvement. Instead of 'Does not concentrate,' or 'Could do better,' it said things like 'Tries hard' and 'Has worked well.'

Now that is not quite all. A few days before Christmas Barbara went home and took all her dolls with her. Bobby was secretly quite sorry to say goodbye to Hans, but he tried not to show it. Then, on Christmas Eve, a parcel arrived for Bobby Brewster, and when he unwrapped it, what do you think he found? Hans, all done up in tissue paper, without any note or letter of explanation. Barbara had never before sent Bobby a Christmas present and he thought it rather peculiar, but of course he wrote her a 'Thank you' letter, and in reply he had an even greater surprise.

This is what it said —

'Dear Bobby,

'Thank you for thanking me for Hans, but I can't understand how he ever got to your home, because I didn't send him there. He must like you so much that he did himself up in a parcel and posted himself, so that proves he is magic, doesn't it?

'Love from Barbara.'

Bobby could not possibly deny that, could he?

66

If you think so, just you try doing yourself up in a parcel and posting yourself. Besides, the next morning something else happened that made it even more certain that Hans is magic.

But please, if you ever meet any of Bobby Brewster's school friends, don't tell them about this, because they might make fun of him, and he doesn't like that. You see, Bobby was so pleased to have Hans back, that he took him to bed with him. And every morning since then Bobby has been wakened up promptly at seven o'clock by the sound of merry yodelling. He has, really!

Now Bobby Brewster can't yodel, and Mr and Mrs Brewster say that even if they could, they would never dream of doing such a thing at seven o'clock in the morning. So there's only one person left to do the yodelling, isn't there?

And that's Hans.

Plum pudding dog

Bobby Brewster comes into this story, but it's really about me, and I'm just H. E. Todd the author of this book. It isn't even a proper story either, because it's about a dream I had the other night. At least, I think it was a dream, but you must make up your own mind about that.

Of course, we've all read things that grown-ups call stories about dreams, haven't we? You know what I mean. They usually end something like this:

'And then Tommy woke up. It had all been a dream, and there he was, in his clean white bed, with no sign of the little red gnomes anywhere.'

No, or any sign of a story either. I think that sort of thing is cheating, don't you? You never know where you are.

Mind you, dreams can be funny things. I expect you sometimes dream at night, don't you? Most people do. It can be very nice and you are really sorry to wake up and find it's not true. Or it can be rather nasty, in which case you are jolly glad to wake up and see your own bedroom. Sometimes it's just silly. So silly that you say to yourself while you are still dreaming, 'This can't be true, it must be just a silly dream.'

But whatever sort of dream it is, as often as not you wake up suddenly, say to yourself, 'Oh what a lovely – or horrid – or silly – dream,' and then find that you can't remember a thing about it.

Not always, though. Just once in a while you have a dream that is so vivid that the details are clear in your mind for quite a long time, and it is that sort of dream that I am writing about now. I hope you don't mind reading about it in a Bobby Brewster book. Anyway, here goes.

Last Tuesday night I went to bed late and fell asleep immediately. As soon as my eyes were closed I found myself standing in the Brewster's kitchen. Bobby Brewster was there, wearing blue and white striped pyjamas of all things, and his mother and father were there too. Mrs Brewster wore a pretty flowered apron, but Mr Brewster was the smartest of all. He was dressed in white chef's uniform with a tall white hat, and he had grown a wide moustache.

'I'm surprised to find you at home in the middle of the day,' I said, and even while I was saying it I thought how silly I was being, because I knew perfectly well it was in the middle of the night and I was dreaming.

'Why should I not be at home?' asked Mr Brewster, and he seemed to have developed a French accent to go with his chef's uniform and big moustache.

70

'Because you're usually out at work,' I replied.

'Not these days,' said Mr Brewster. 'This *is* my work. I'm now an expert at cooking plum pudding dogs.'

'I beg your pardon?' I asked. 'Surely you mean plum puddings?'

'No, I don't,' said Mr Brewster. 'I said plum pudding dogs. Anyone with a little suet and some flour and fruit and things can boil a plum pudding, but I'm the only man in the world who can boil a plum pudding *dog*.'

'Indeed,' I said, and I'm afraid I didn't believe him.

Then I looked over to the stove. On it was a large saucepan with steam pouring from under the lid.

'Let me show you,' said Mr Brewster. 'It must be very nearly done by now,' and he carefully lifted the lid with a cloth. Inside the saucepan, standing in boiling water, was a bowl covered with muslin, which was tied round the rim with string.

'Listen,' said Mr Brewster, as he prodded inside the muslin cover with a fork.

All I could hear at first was the boiling of the water and the hissing of the steam, but then, quite distinctly, the pudding underneath the cover started to bark. It did, really!

'That's right,' said Mr Brewster. 'That means it *is* done.' He carried the saucepan over to the sink, emptied the boiling water, took out the bowl, cut the string with a knife, and removed the muslin. Over the top of one side of the bowl shot a plum pudding tail, and over the top of the other side peeped a surprised plum pudding face.

For a moment everything was quite still. Then

the look of surprise on the plum pudding face turned to one of excitement, the tail started wagging, and a complete plum pudding dog jumped to the ground, ran along the kitchen floor, and bounded on to Bobby Brewster's lap.

'Look what Father's given me,' said Bobby Brewster, grinning all over his face. 'And can you guess what *I'm* going to call him?'

'No,' I said.

'Suet!' said Bobby Brewster.

I thought it was rather a peculiar name for a dog, even a plum pudding dog, but before I had time to say so I woke up.

Well – so far, so good. I wondered what on earth had made me dream such ridiculous things and then thought no more about it. But on Thursday evening I happened to be near the Brewster's home and thought I would take the opportunity of calling on them. I do from time to time, you know, in case Bobby Brewster can tell me about any more of his extraordinary adventures.

Mrs Brewster came to the door when I rang

the bell. She was wearing a pretty flowered overall.

'Hullo,' she said. 'I *am* glad to see you. And you're just in time to catch Bobby before he goes to bed. He has something to show you.'

I went into the sitting-room. There was Bobby Brewster, dressed in blue and white striped pyjamas, and on his lap was a very cheerful-looking plum pudding dog, wagging his tail furiously.

'Look what Father's given me,' said Bobby Brewster, grinning all over his face. 'And can you guess what I'm going to call him?'

'Suet,' I said.

'How on earth did you know?' asked Bobby Brewster in great surprise.

Well – how *did* I know?

School pantomime

Mr Limcano is very popular with all the boys at Miss Trenham's school. Of course, they make fun of him behind his back sometimes, and call him 'Old Limmy,' when he isn't listening, but that only goes to show that they like him, doesn't it?

His lessons are interesting too. I suppose that is hardly to be wondered at when he is being magical, but he even manages to make ordinary lessons interesting, because he is always full of new ideas.

He had one of his best ideas at the beginning of last winter term. 'Boys,' he announced, 'I've made a suggestion to Miss Trenham to which she has readily agreed. Instead of having the usual Christmas concert this term we're going to produce a pantomime.'

'What, a real pantomime, sir, with costumes and scenery?' asked Willie Watson.

'Yes,' said Mr Limcano. 'I'm writing it myself and it's nearly finished. It'll be called *Aladdin and the Two Genii*.'

'How super, sir!' cried the boys. 'When are we going to start?'

'I'll hold an audition next Tuesday afternoon after school,' said Mr Limcano. 'So, in the meantime, I suggest you all practice by reading aloud to yourselves whenever the opportunity occurs.'

Well, some extraordinary scenes could be seen all over the place for the next few days. During break periods, Billy Singleton, who is rather proud of his low, gruff voice, kept folding his arms and announcing in ringing tones, 'I am the genie of the lamp. What dost thou command?'

He seemed quite annoyed when at last one of the boys replied, 'I command you to shut up and stop playing the fool.' Willie Watson, who is rather a small boy, fancied his chances as a princess, and tried walking about with short steps, talking in a squeaky voice, and doing wobbly curtsies.

As for Bobby Brewster, he quite worried his mother. She couldn't understand why he often stood in front of his bedroom mirror waving his arms and making funny faces. When he started talking loudly to himself in bed, she almost decided to call in the doctor, but luckily the next day she heard about the pantomime from one of the other mothers and changed her mind.

When Tuesday afternoon came there was great excitement at Miss Trenham's. Mr Limcano sat in the school hall and asked the boys who were trying for parts to go on the stage and repeat speeches after him. Funny speeches they were, too, all in rhyme. Bobby Brewster felt an awful fool when he had to say to Willie Watson —

'Princess, I've loved you all my life
And want you now to be my wife.'

And Willie Watson felt even more of a fool when he had to reply —

'My heart is pounding while I speak.
I'll marry you next Tuesday week.'

They must have spoken their lines convincingly, though, because when the list of parts was posted on the school notice-board the next day, this is what it said:

Cast for *ALADDIN AND THE TWO GENII*

Aladdin	Bobby Brewster
Princess Fatima	Willie Watson
Dandini	John Willis
King of Persia	Alisdair Cameron
Queen of Persia	Angus Cameron
Widow Twanky	Percy Caldicott
Ebeneezer	Harry Walker
Genie of the Ring, and Genie of the Lamp	Billy Singleton

Then there was a list of palace attendants, townspeople and ladies of the chorus too long to mention here.

Well, the rehearsals were all most enthusiastic.

Mr Limcano was a very patient producer. He needed to be, especially when the boys forgot their lines and the ladies of the chorus banged into each other during the Eastern dances. Gradually, however, they improved, and after a successful dress rehearsal everyone was full of confidence. But on the morning of the first performance a very sad thing happened. Billy Singleton was absent and his mother sent a note. This is what it said:

'Dear Mr Limcano,

'I am sorry to tell you that Billy woke up this morning covered with spots and the doctor says he has measles and must stay in bed. I cannot tell you how *sorry he is to miss the pantomime and I hope you can arrange for someone else to play the parts.*

'*Yours sincerely,*

'*Sheila Singleton.*'

Well, that was a fine thing, wasn't it? *Aladdin and the Two Genii* without a single genie in it would be ridiculous. None of the other boys knew the parts, and in any case Billy Singleton is so fat that his costumes would have looked silly on anyone else. Mr Limcano had almost decided to take the two parts himself, when a very funny thing happened.

Bobby Brewster had gone all alone to the hall to practise handling the magic lamp, which was rather an awkward shape. He picked it up and gave it a jolly good rub when there was a green flash, and standing next to him was a little man with a drooping moustache dressed in a green uniform and with a green turban on his head. There was, really!

'What dost thou command, oh great and wonderful master?' asked the little man in a feeble voice.

'I beg your pardon?' asked Bobby Brewster.

'I said, what dost thou command, oh great and wonderful master?' repeated the little man.

'Haven't we met before somewhere?' asked Bobby Brewster, looking at him more closely.

'Yes,' said the little man. 'I was hoping you'd forgotten. I was the genie of the gong at the Townley House Hotel. Do you remember?'

'Indeed I do,' said Bobby Brewster. 'Isn't your name Wilfred?'

'Yes. Wilfred Snoxall,' said the little man.

'What are you doing here?' asked Bobby Brewster.

'Well, as you know,' said Wilfred, 'I went back to the genie school after that mix up with the food at the Townley House Hotel. Since then I've worked hard for two terms, but they still won't trust me as a real genie, so this Christmas time I'm being tried out as an understudy for any pantomime genii who fall ill. That's why I appeared when you rubbed the lamp.'

'What a lucky thing,' said Bobby Brewster.

'Well, you may think so,' said Wilfred, 'but

my memory is still bad for a genie, I'm afraid.'

'Never mind about that,' said Bobby Brewster. 'Mr Limcano will be delighted. I'm sure that he'll say that any genie is better than no genie.'

Bobby Brewster was quite right. Mr Limcano was absolutely delighted. At first he was surprised, of course, but, as you know, he is more used to magic than most people, so he soon got over his surprise.

'There's no need for you to learn the part,' he said to Wilfred. 'You can say whatever comes into your head, and after all, since you are a real under-study genie, you'll be able to make things appear when people on the stage ask for them, won't you, Wilfred?'

'Er – I hope so, sir,' said Wilfred – but he didn't sound very sure of himself.

Before the performance that evening Mr Limcano

went on the stage to make an announcement. 'Ladies and gentlemen,' he said. 'Owing to the unfortunate illness of Billy Singleton, the parts of the Genie of the Ring and the Genie of the Lamp will be taken at very short notice by Wilfred Snoxall.'

There was a sympathetic murmur in the audience, and people clapped Wilfred Snoxall for helping out at the last moment.

The early scenes of the pantomime went very well. Willie Watson was clapped loudly for singing a song called 'Princesses have a lonely life', and Percy Caldicott made everyone laugh when he was hanging out the washing. But it was the first appearance of the Genie of the Ring in the cave that caused the most astonishment. People wondered how on earth Mr Limcano had managed to arrange for such an impressive puff of green smoke. Of course, they didn't realize that it was real genie smoke. There stood the Genie of the Ring, surrounded by green smoke and in full green uniform, and they clapped loud and long.

Now Wilfred Snoxall isn't used to crowds or noise. He usually appears when only one person is about. All the clapping made him completely tongue-tied and instead of saying 'What dost thou command' he just stood there with his drooping moustache shaking with stage fright.

Bobby Brewster as Aladdin thought he had better ask a question of his own in pantomime language just to help things along, so he said to the genie, 'Who art thou?'

'I'm Wilfred Snoxall,' said the genie, which made all the audience laugh and the poor genie even more confused.

'Why hast thou appeared?' asked Aladdin.

'I don't know. I've forgotten,' said the poor genie, and the audience laughed louder than ever.

'Canst use thy magic to free me from this cave?' asked Aladdin helpfully.

'I'll try,' said the Genie.

Well, he did – and it didn't! He must have said the magic word the wrong way round, because the result was that the entrance to the cave was jammed tight and no one, not even the genie himself, could get off the stage. In the end they had to climb over the footlights and out of a side entrance, while the scene shifters came into the hall and removed the cave scene through the front of the curtains.

After that things went from bad to worse. Poor Wilfred Snoxall was in such a state that he did nothing right. When Aladdin rubbed his ring the Genie of the Lamp would appear, and the only way to summon the Genie of the Ring was to find the lamp and give it a jolly good rub. The love scene between Aladdin and the Princess was

completely ruined. The genie of the lamp suddenly appeared for no reason at all during the marriage proposal. When they asked him to disappear again he said half the password and only his top half disappeared. So they had to continue their love-making in the presence of a pair of legs wearing green trousers with a hole being burned in the seat, which made it very difficult either for them or the audience to take the scene seriously.

The only thing that Wilfred always managed without fail was to make a large cloud of green smoke when he appeared and disappeared, and even that he overdid. He was on and off so many times that the hall was filled with green smoke. What with the audience roaring with laughter and blinded with green smoke, it was very difficult either to see or hear what was happening on the stage.

Poor Mr Limcano was frantic – but he needn't have worried. You see, the audience still didn't know it was all a mistake, and they thought the funny things were really supposed to be happening. When the show was over – which was rather earlier than had been expected – they all trooped out with eyes streaming with green smoke and tears of laughter, and assured Mr Limcano that his idea of using two forgetful genii who mixed everything up was one of the funniest things they had ever seen. So Mr Limcano had all the credit for a pantomime that happened by mistake, and he was wise enough not to say any more about it.

As a matter of fact this story has a double happy ending. Mr Limcano was not the only one who went home happy that night. When they were undressing after the show, some of the boys felt rather disappointed because they hadn't been able to say their lines properly in all the confusion. Bobby Brewster was wondering how he could cheer them up when he had an idea. He rubbed the magic lamp again.

There was a puff of green smoke and Wilfred Snoxall appeared as the Genie of the Ring.

'I should like the boys to have a jolly good feed,' said Bobby Brewster. 'Please get four jugs of lemonade and lots of sardine sandwiches.'

'I'll try,' said Wilfred. 'Just give me five

minutes and then rub something. It doesn't matter whether it's your ring or the lamp.'

The five minutes soon passed, and then Bobby rubbed both ring and lamp just to make sure. I think that must have doubled the magic, because when Wilfred reappeared in another puff of green smoke he was carrying a very heavy tray with eight jugs of lemonade and a pile of sandwiches which nearly reached the ceiling. It was a jolly good thing that Bobby was ready to catch hold of the tray too, because, before he finally disappeared, Wilfred very nearly dropped it and smashed the lot.

Further adventures with Bobby Brewster